The Lord's Prayer In Korean
Colouring Book

The Beautiful, Simple to Colour Characters
of the Korean Language

주여님의 기도
채색 도서

MAGDALENE PRESS

The Lord's Prayer in Korean Colouring Book
The Beautiful, Simple to Colour Characters of the Korean Language
by Esther Pincini

주님 의기도
채색 도서

Copyright © Magdalene Press 2018

ISBN 978-1-77335-114-8

No part of this publication may be reproduced, stored in a retrieval system, or transmitted in any form or by any means, electronic, mechanical, photocopying, recording or otherwise without written permission of the publisher.

Magdalene Press, 2018

식

Here is the Lord's Prayer in Korean with translations and transliterations:

하늘에 계신 우리 아버지
Our Father who art in heaven

하늘에 (in heaven) 계신 (formal "is" - "who art") 우리 (our) 아버지 (father) (haneul-eh gyeshin oori ahbeoji)

아버지의 이름이 거룩하게 하시며
Hallowed by thy name

아버지의 (Father's) 이름이 (name) 거룩하게 (Holy) 하시며 (be)   (ahbeojiui ireumi golukhagey hasimyo)

아버지의 나라가 오게 하시며
Thy kingdom come

아버지의 (Father's) 나라가 (Kingdom) 오게 (come) 하시며 (be)   (ahbeojiui naraga ohgey hasimyo)

아버지의 뜻이 하늘에서와 같이 땅에서도 이루어지게 하소서
Thy will be done on earth as it is in heaven

아버지의 (Father's) 뜻이 (will) 하늘에서와 (in heaven) 같이 (together with)   (ahbeojiui ddeusi haneul-eh-sau-wah gatch-ee)

땅에서도 (on earth also) 이루어지게 (accomplish) 하소서 (will be)   (ddang-eh-doh ilueojige hasoseo)

오늘 우리에게 필요한 양식을 주시고
Give us this day our daily bread

오늘 (today) 우리에게 (our) 필요한 (needed) 양식을 (daily food) 주시고 (please give) (oneul uliege pil-yohan yangsig-eul jusigo)

우리가 우리에게 잘못한 일를 용서하듯이
Forgive us our trespasses

우리가 (Us) 우리에게 (our) 잘못한 이를 (trespasses) 용서하듯이 (forgive as) (uliga uliege jalmotan ileul yongseohadeus-i)

우리의 잘못을 용서하시고
as we forgive those who trespass against us

우리의 (our) 잘못을 (trespasses) 용서하시고 (forgive) (uliui jalmos-eul yongseohasigo)

우리를 유혹에 빠지지 않게 하시고
Lead us not into temptation

우리를 (us) 유혹에 (into temptation) 빠지지 (not led into) 않게 하시고 (ulileul yuhog-e ppajiji anhge hasigo)

악에서 구하소서
and deliver us from evil.

악에서 (from evil) 구하소서 (deliver) (ag-eseo guhasoseo)

www.ingramcontent.com/pod-product-compliance
Lightning Source LLC
Chambersburg PA
CBHW051120110526
44589CB00026B/2985